A Note From Rick Renner

I am on a personal quest to see a "revival of the Bible" so people can establish their lives on a firm foundation that will stand strong and endure the test as end-time storm winds begin to intensify.

In order to experience a revival of the Bible in your personal life, it is important to take time each day to read, receive, and apply its truths to your life. James tells us that if we will continue in the perfect law of liberty — refusing to be forgetful hearers, but determined to be doers — we will be blessed in our ways. As you watch or listen to the programs in this series and work through this corresponding study guide, I trust you will search the Scriptures and allow the Holy Spirit to help you hear something new from God's Word that applies specifically to your life. I encourage you to be a doer of the Word He reveals to you. Whatever the cost, I assure you — it will be worth it.

> Thy words were found, and I did eat them;
> and thy word was unto me the joy and rejoicing of mine heart:
> for I am called by thy name, O Lord God of hosts.
> — Jeremiah 15:16

Your brother and friend in Jesus Christ,

Rick Renner

You Are the Light of the World

Copyright © 2025 by Rick Renner
1814 W. Tacoma St.
Broken Arrow, OK 74012-1406

Published by Rick Renner Ministries
www.renner.org

ISBN 13: 978-1-6675-1157-3

ISBN 13 eBook: 978-1-6675-1158-0

How To Use This Study Guide

This five-lesson study guide corresponds to *"You Are the Light of the World" With Rick Renner* (Renner TV). Each lesson in this study guide covers a topic that is addressed during the program series, with questions and references supplied to draw you deeper into your own private study of the Scriptures on this subject.

To derive the most benefit from this study guide, consider the following:

First, watch or listen to the program prior to working through the corresponding lesson in this guide. (Programs can also be viewed at **renner.org** by clicking on the Media/Archives links or on our Renner Ministries YouTube channel.)

Second, take the time to look up the scriptures included in each lesson. Prayerfully consider their application to your own life.

Third, use a journal or notebook to make note of your answers to each lesson's Study Questions and Practical Application challenges.

Fourth, invest specific time in prayer and in the Word of God to consult with the Holy Spirit. Write down the scriptures or insights He reveals to you.

Finally, take action! Whatever the Lord tells you to do according to His Word, do it.

For added insights on this subject, it is recommended that you obtain Rick Renner's book *Easter — the Rest of the Story* and *Christmas — The Rest of the Story*. You may also select from Rick's other available resources by placing your order at **renner.org** or by calling 1-800-742-5593.

TOPIC

You Are the Light of the World

SCRIPTURES

1. **Matthew 5:14** — Ye are the light of the world. A city that is set on an hill cannot be hid.

2. **Matthew 5:16** — Let your light so shine before men, that they may see your good works, and glorify your Father which is in heaven.

GREEK WORDS

No Greek words were shown on the TV program.

SYNOPSIS

The five lessons in this study titled *You Are the Light of the World* will focus on the following topics:

- You Are the Light of the World
- You've Got What It Takes
- Quit Badgering Yourself
- Guts and Gumption
- You Are Golden

In Matthew 5:14, Jesus declared, "Ye are the light of the world. A city that is set on an hill cannot be hid." There is much to be learned from these insightful words, and in these five lessons, we will unpack the rich meaning of what the Lord said and how it applies to our lives today.

The emphasis of this lesson:

When Jesus called us as believers the "light of the world," He was remembering and comparing us to the powerful influence of the city of Sepphoris just to the north of Nazareth. Like Sepphoris, we are to be a glistening beacon of light, shining in the darkness of people's lives all around us.

The Remarkable City of Sepphoris

Just a three-mile walk from the town of Nazareth is an ancient city called Sepphoris — a city so elegant in ancient times, it was known as "the ornament of Galilee." At night, you could look across the valley from the ridge of Nazareth and see Sepphoris up on a hill. This is the city Jesus was referring to when He said, "Ye are the light of the world. A city that is set on an hill cannot be hid" (Matthew 5:14).

This remarkable city became the center of trade and commerce in the northern region of Israel, and it was one of the largest banking centers of the Middle East. Because of Sepphoris' extreme wealth, it had facilities that would normally be associated only with larger cities, such as a huge theater that seated 5,000 people and had a constant array of dramatic presentations. Most Jewish cities in Israel did not have a theater.

Sepphoris also had scores of beautiful upper-class villas to accommodate the wealthy people who lived there, and it was adorned with some of the finest mosaics that existed in the First Century. In fact, the synagogue in Sepphoris was decked out with the most elaborate mosaics anywhere in the ancient world. Even today one can see some of the finest examples of early mosaics lying in the ancient ruins of Sepphoris.

This city was exquisite in every way, featuring a triumphant arch, an aqueduct, multiple palaces, huge entrance gates, and several pagan temples. Sepphoris was so splendid it influenced the entire region of Galilee. Sophisticated and wealthy, it attracted visitors from around the world. Every day one could experience a wide range of different cultures, ethnic groups, and customs. People could be heard speaking Greek, Hebrew, and Aramaic in the streets. It was a tri-lingual city known for being open-minded and for having an emphasis on learning, education, and business.

Although the city of Sepphoris dates to Greek times, it was enhanced at the orders of Herod Antipas concurrent to the time Jesus was growing up just three miles away in Nazareth during the First Century. Nazareth was one of five small villages surrounding Sepphoris, and like the other villages, it was occupied mostly by workers who were employed in the enhancement of rebuilding this fabulous, wealthy city that was the northern home and administrative center for Herod Antipas.

As a 'Carpenter,'
Joseph Was a Highly Skilled Craftsman

The Bible tells us Joseph, Jesus' earthly father, was a *carpenter* (*see* Matthew 13:55). In Greek, the word "carpenter" is from a form of the word *tekton*, which describes *a highly skilled craftsman*. It is where we get the words *technician* and *technology*.

What's interesting about the word *tekton* is that rather than working with wood, a *tekton* worked with silver, gold, ivory, precious metals, and stone. Thus, a *tekton* could be a stone mason, a construction engineer, or even a construction-site supervisor, and anyone who was a *tekton* was handsomely paid.

Considering the likelihood that a little town such as Nazareth would not have much work available for a man with these skills, it is likely Joseph — an extremely skilled craftsman — was involved in the high level of construction taking place in nearby Sepphoris. Therefore, it is highly possible that Joseph walked the three miles from Nazareth to Sepphoris each day and worked as a highly paid, advanced technological worker. This shows that he was not poor as many have traditionally taught.

It also appears likely that Mary's father worked as a scroll keeper in the synagogue in Sepphoris. The fact that Jesus' earthly father, Joseph, may have worked in Sepphoris and His grandparents may have lived there tells us that Jesus probably made regular trips from Nazareth to Sepphoris to see His father and spend time with His grandparents.

Jesus Was Greatly Influenced
by the Lifestyle and Activities of Sepphoris

It was most likely during Jesus' time in Sepphoris that He was exposed to many amazing things — things He would have never experienced while growing up in Nazareth. In Sepphoris, He could become familiar and comfortable with words, phrases, and knowledge that would not be customary for a boy from a small and obscure village to know.

For example, when Jesus came to Sepphoris, He was exposed to the theater, including the fact that the actors who wore masks were called *hypocrites*. When He taught during His ministry years, He used many theatrical terms and examples from the theater — which did not exist in Nazareth, but did exist in Sepphoris.

Likewise, Jesus was exposed to the banking industry, enabling Him to be familiar with banking terms and the movement of massive amounts of money — something a village boy would know nothing about unless he had seen it somewhere. During His ministry, He spoke in such terms when He related His stories.

Moreover, in the city of Sepphoris, Jesus was exposed to how the rich and powerful lived. From the luxurious palaces of politicians to the sophisticated art and culture of the learned, Jesus became well acquainted with the terminology and real-life dynamics of the wealthy that could not be acquired in Nazareth. In ministry, He spoke of governmental authorities as if He had personal knowledge of the subject — a level of knowledge He could have only attained by observation at nearby Sepphoris.

Even the three-mile journey between Nazareth and Sepphoris was providential. As He walked that territory again and again, Jesus observed agricultural areas and learned about farming techniques that He would draw from for years to come.

When you read what Jesus taught in the four gospels, you can see that He drew on all these different areas of experience and wove aspects of what He learned and observed firsthand into all the parables He taught. Where did a boy from Nazareth learn so much about wealth and commerce, the banking industry, art and the theater, and the luxurious lifestyle of the upper class? It was in the nearby town of Sepphoris. Because His father likely worked there and his grandparents lived there, Jesus regularly visited the city as a child and was exposed to all these things.

The city of Sepphoris — a "city set on a hill" — had a great influence on the life of Jesus from His early childhood and during the time He was growing up as a small boy. Living under the influence of that city helped to form His worldview and His appreciation of different cultures. It gave Him a broad enough experience to venture far beyond Nazareth and speak authoritatively to people on every level of life.

Developing Well-Rounded Children
Is Vital for Them To Be the Light of the World

Everyone in Galilee fell under the influence of the city of Sepphoris —
including Jesus. If He and His parents stood on the ridge of Nazareth
and looked northwest across the valley, they would see an acropolis in
the distance along with all the gleaming, glistening lights of the city of
Sepphoris.

If the atmospheric conditions were just right, they may have even been able
to hear the music and smell the smells coming from Sepphoris. What this
tells us is that God the Father wanted to be certain His Son was exposed
to many wonderful things so that He would be equipped and prepared to
speak to people on every level of life.

As a parent or grandparent, make sure your children and grandchildren
develop a well-rounded, healthy worldview. This comes from providing
them with a good, Christ-centered education. There's a lot of bad education out there, so pray and explore the options that are available where you
live.

At the right time and in the right way, expose them to things like the
banking industry, politics, and the lifestyles of the upper class as well as
the poor. Teach them about art, sculpture, music, and sophistication. If
you make sure they are well-rounded, it will be a blessing to them and
to others because they'll be equipped to speak to anyone they come in
contact with in life, which is so very important.

Be Like the City of Sepphoris —
Shine Your Light Wherever You Go!

Looking again at Matthew 5:14, Jesus said, "Ye are the light of the world.
A city that is set on an hill cannot be hid." No doubt, when Jesus spoke
these words to His followers, He saw the city of Sepphoris in His mind
and remembered the strong, influential role it played in His life and the
lives of all the people living in the region of Galilee.

Jesus went on to say, "Let your light so shine before men, that they may see
your good works, and glorify your Father which is in heaven" (Matthew 5:16).
Essentially, Jesus is telling us that just as the city of Sepphoris was a city on a
hill that could not be hidden, we are to stand out in our sphere of influence.

We are to be individuals who are so well-developed that we shine the light of Jesus wherever we go.

Friend, God saved you, redeemed you, delivered you, and filled you with the light of His Word. Don't be ashamed of what He has done in you. Instead, let that light shine brightly so it can penetrate the darkness in others and give them light to guide them through the night they're experiencing right now in their lives.

If you're like most people, you've probably spent a great deal of time putting yourself down and badgering yourself about your failures — you may have even been tempted to largely forget about the great work God has done in your life. If so, it's time for you to put an end to that downward spiral.

Stop berating yourself over your missteps and start thanking God for the progress you've already made! Then reach out to someone else in need so you can become a godly influence to benefit them. That person can be touched, changed, and shaped by the light in your life.

Right now, there are people observing you and taking note of the light that is shining in your life. You may not be aware of it, but that person or group of people is watching the way you live, how you act, what you do, and what kind of excellence and attitude you demonstrate in your life. They are watching you — and you are making an impact on their lives.

What an opportunity you've been given to become a godly influence on someone who really needs your example. So, continue your walk of obedience! As you lean on the Holy Spirit and do your best to obey Him, the light He has placed in you will begin to shine into someone else's darkness and bring about the hope and change for which they long.

STUDY QUESTIONS

> **Study to shew thyself approved unto God, a workman that needeth not to be ashamed, rightly dividing the word of truth.**
> **— 2 Timothy 2:15**

1. Prior to this lesson, had you ever heard of the ancient city of Sepphoris? What new facts about this exquisite Galilean hub did you learn? How do these important details help you better understand Jesus and His family and how His life was shaped during His growing years?

2. When you consider the meaning of the word "carpenter," which is from the Greek word *tekton*, how does it enlarge your view of Joseph, the earthly father of Jesus?

PRACTICAL APPLICATION

> **But be ye doers of the word, and not hearers only,**
> **deceiving your own selves.**
> **— James 1:22**

1. In this lesson, we learned some important details of Jesus' formative years. What were *your* growing years like? In what city and region did you live, and how did it influence and affect your worldview and the person you are today? Pray and ask the Holy Spirit to pull back the curtain so you can see what you need to know in order to *grow forward* into God's plan for your life.
2. As a parent or grandparent, are you actively involved in your children's and grandchildren's lives? In what specific ways are you helping them develop a healthy, well-rounded worldview? Is there anything you sense the Holy Spirit is nudging you to change? If so, what is it?
3. What kind of influence are you having on the people around you? Is it positive? Are you using the things you've been taught and the lessons you've learned from life's experiences to reach others for Jesus?

LESSON 2

TOPIC

You've Got What It Takes

SCRIPTURES

1. **Matthew 5:15** — Neither do men light a candle, and put it under a bushel, but on a candlestick; and it giveth light unto all that are in the house.

GREEK WORDS

1. "candle" — λύχνος (*luchnos*): an oil-burning lamp that is carried by hand, positioned on a table, or elevated on a stand; such lamps were fashioned of earthen clay with a reservoir to hold oil and a wick that gave light in darkness once it was lit; oil-burning lamps were vital to life because they were the only source of light in darkness

SYNOPSIS

Have you ever wondered if you had what it takes to live a godly life and do what God has asked you to do? If so, wonder no more! The Bible says, "By his divine power, God has given us *everything* we need for living a godly life. We have received all of this by coming to know him, the one who called us to himself by means of his marvelous glory and excellence" (2 Peter 1:3 *NLT*).

Regardless of the enemy's condemning thoughts that come against your mind or the negative feelings you may have felt toward yourself, God is most definitely *for you*, and you've got what it takes to do anything and everything He has called you to do!

The emphasis of this lesson:

Jesus called us the *light of the world* and compared us to a First Century, oil-burning lamp. As God's lamp, we are fashioned to contain the oil of the Holy Spirit and burn brightly and continuously with His fire, bringing light and godly influence everywhere we go.

The Meaning of the Word 'Candle' and Rick's Discovery of Ancient 'Lamps'

Immediately after Jesus declared that we are the "light of the world" in Matthew 5:14, He then added, "Neither do men light a candle, and put it under a bushel, but on a candlestick; and it giveth light unto all that are in the house" (Matthew 5:15). Now when most people in the western world hear the word *candle*, they immediately think of a cylindrical-shaped candle made of wax with a wick that runs through the center. But that is not what Jesus was referring to in this passage.

The word "candle" here is a form of the Greek word *luchnos*, and it describes *an oil-burning lamp that is carried by hand, positioned on a table, or elevated on a stand.* Rick has always been fascinated by such relics of the past, which is why on one of his trips to Israel, he took a break from his speaking schedule to visit a local archaeologist's office to view firsthand what these ancient lamps looked like. Here is what he shared about his exciting adventure:

> As I waited for the archaeologist to pull those rare lamps out of a box so I could examine them, I was amazed at how many he had collected. There were scores of them — and he let me know that what he had was just the tip of the iceberg compared to the large collection he had put away in storage.
>
> When he saw the surprised look on my face, he began to explain how the soil of Israel is loaded with archaeological relics, including ancient oil lamps. He said, 'There are so many of these in the ground that you can dig just about anywhere, and eventually you'll find an oil lamp.'
>
> 'Really?' I asked. 'After thousands of years have passed, I thought these would be pretty rare. Why are there still so many of them being found?'
>
> The archaeologist answered, 'In the First Century, these oil-based lamps were the only source of light in the ancient world. As you can see, these lamps aren't very large. If a person really wanted to light his house or business, he had to use many of them throughout all his many rooms. That's why there is still such an abundance of them scattered in the dirt throughout the land of Israel.'
>
> As I reached out and took one of the lamps in my hand, the archaeologist said, 'That's a Herodian lamp from the time of Herod the Great. It dates to the days of Jesus.' It was small, formed of clay, and shaped to hold oil inside. It had a small opening or spout at the end, which is often called the mouth, where a wick could be inserted into the base of the lamp to soak up oil.
>
> In ancient days, when it was time to light a lamp like this, fire was put to the wick, and it burned steadily because it was saturated with oil from inside. The opening on the very top of the lamp enabled it to be refilled again and again. As long as oil was supplied, it would keep burning and giving light.

Today that Herodian lamp sits on the shelf in Rick's studio in Moscow, and he said in the program that every time he stops to look at it, his mind goes to Jesus' words in Matthew 5:15.

The Structure and Use of First Century Oil Lamps

Looking once more at Jesus' words, He said, "Neither do men light a candle, and put it under a bushel, but on a candlestick; and it giveth light unto all that are in the house" (Matthew 5:15). Again, the word "candle" is from a form of the Greek word *luchnos*, and it depicts *an oil-burning lamp that is carried by hand, positioned on a table, or elevated on a stand.*

Oil-burning lamps like these were used by Jews, Greeks, and Byzantine Christians who lived in the era of the Roman Empire. The basic construction and function of these lamps was the same across all cultures. Each one had a hole in the top for refilling, a reservoir to hold oil, and a wick that went down into a spout at the end that could be lit.

These oil lamps were vital to life because they were the only source of light in darkness. A literal translation of this part of Matthew 5:15 would be: "Neither do men light an oil lamp and put it under a bushel…." In this text, Jesus was exhorting the disciples — and *us* — to be just like one of these ancient oil lamps. We are fashioned by God to let our light shine before men so we can influence the world around us.

Jesus used the example of an oil lamp to make a point, so before we proceed any further, we will focus on why Jesus used an oil lamp and why this imagery is such a perfect illustration of us!

Oil Lamps Were Everywhere

In Matthew 5:14, Jesus declared, "You are the light of the world," and then in verse 15 compared us with an oil-burning lamp — the Greek word *luchnos* translated here as "candle." This "candle" wasn't like our wax-filled candles today, but instead it was a lamp hand-fashioned from earthen clay and was small enough to be carried in the palm of one's hand. It was designed to hold oil and had a long wick that — once saturated — could be ignited to illuminate darkness.

As stated before, it was often carried by hand, positioned on a table, or elevated on a stand. Hence, the *luchnos* was a very important part of daily life in the First Century. Every building in that period — from the smallest house to the greatest palace — depended on oil-burning lamps to provide light. Every house, apartment, store, and place of business in the ancient world had at least one oil-burning lamp — if not many. This is one reason these ancient lamps are often discovered in great numbers in archeological excavations.

It is also important to note that these clay lamps were so very fragile and brittle that they could be broken by the mere squeeze of a hand. Anyone carrying one of these lamps had to be careful not to break it, because — if it broke — the oil would spill out and the light the lamp provided would be lost.

The Spiritual Parallels
Between Us and Oil Lamps

Jesus said we are just like these lamps! We, too, are made of clay — formed from the "dust of the ground" (Genesis 2:7). As the Church and as individuals, we are imperfect human beings in so many ways. Emotionally and physically, we are very fragile, and if we are mishandled, sometimes we can break.

Who could have ever imagined that God would put His Spirit in a vessel so fragile as a human body or in a Church made up of very imperfect people! Nevertheless, God chose *us* — the Church — as His primary instrument for giving His light to a dark world. Just as the lamps were carried by hand from room to room, we are carried in Jesus' hand and directed by Him to bring light and dispel darkness everywhere we go.

Oil represents the Holy Spirit. These earthen lamps contained oil, which was extremely valuable and never wasted. Oil is a symbol of the Holy Spirit in both the Old and New Testaments, and just as these oil-burning lamps contained oil, the Church is the container of the priceless Holy Spirit in this world. Although it is true that the weaknesses of God's people are readily evident, He has graciously chosen to deposit the oil of the Holy Spirit within us with the intention and desire that this divine oil will extend His life-giving light to the very ends of the earth.

Every lamp had a wick in its mouth. For the oil in these lamps to provide light, a wick was required. The wick was inserted into the mouth of the lamp and ran deep into its base where it was saturated with oil. When the lamp's wick was lit, it would burn and give light for many hours or even days before the lamp needed to be refilled again.

We, too, have a mouth, and the wick represents our tongue. God has designed us to declare His mighty Word and express who He is through what we speak with our mouth. Jesus said, "…Out of the abundance of the heart the mouth speaketh" (Matthew 12:34). That is why He wants our entire being flooded and filled with His Holy Spirit. When we are drenched inside with the oil of the Spirit, our tongue can be set ablaze with His fire, bringing continuous light to everyone around us.

Every lamp had a reservoir to store oil. When a lamp began to run out of oil, someone would bring a small vase that was filled with oil, which was called a *glutus*, and they would pour more oil into the opening of the lamp. Thus, the lamp had the ability to never run out of oil, because it could regularly be refilled without interrupting the light it was emitting.

In the same way, we've been given the Holy Spirit, and when we feel like we're running low on strength, we can come into the Lord's presence for a fresh infilling of His 'oil.' During our time of fellowship with Him, we can say, "Jesus, I need You to give me a fresh dose of the Holy Ghost." Amazingly, just as oil-burning lamps could regularly be refilled with new oil, we've been designed by God to receive filling after filling, so we never need to run out of the precious oil of the Holy Spirit.

Our job is to get into the presence of God and allow the Holy Spirit to fill us and refill us, again and again. This is what Paul meant when he said, "…Ever be filled and stimulated with the [Holy] Spirit" (Ephesians 5:18 *AMPC*). As we make time to regularly be refilled, we will always have sufficient oil to bring light to people who are in darkness.

God Knows Everything About You and He Loves You Immensely!

Now, you may be thinking, *I just don't know if the Lord would use me. My gifts are not that great, and I seem to keep messing up all the time.* If thoughts like these are running through your head, they are not from God but from the enemy. The Bible says, "…God is so rich in mercy, and he loved us so much, that even though we were dead because of our sins, he gave us life when he raised Christ from the dead. (It is only by God's grace that you have been saved!" Ephesians 2:4,5 *NLT*).

God chose you to be His own, washed you in the blood of Jesus, and filled you with His Holy Spirit — and it is *all by His grace*! Your attitudes and actions are no surprise to God. Before you were born, He knew every thought you would ever think, every word you would ever speak, and every action you would ever make. He watched you be formed in your mother's womb, and knew every day of your life before even one of them took place (*see* Psalm 139:1-4, 13-16).

Friend, God knows everything about you — and yet He still loves you with an immense, everlasting love! He has chosen you to be a carrier of the oil of His Spirit and bring light to those around you. So, stop badgering yourself about past failures and the flaws you see, and receive His unconditional love and acceptance. If you've messed up, fess up. Simply go to God and confess your sin, and He will be faithful to forgive you of your sin and cleanse you of all unrighteousness (*see* 1 John 1:9).

In our next lesson, we will learn what Jesus meant when He said that we are not to put our light "…under a bushel, but on a candlestick; and it giveth light unto all that are in the house" (Matthew 5:15).

STUDY QUESTIONS

**Study to shew thyself approved unto God, a workman that needeth not to be ashamed, rightly dividing the word of truth.
— 2 Timothy 2:15**

1. One of the most important takeaways from this series is that YOU are a container and carrier of the Holy Spirit! To really help you get this truth down deep in your spirit and soul, check out First Corinthians 3:16; 6:19; and Second Corinthians 6:16 — each of which declares that you are the temple of the Holy Spirit. Also consider John 14:17; Romans 8:11,15, and 16; First Corinthians 2:12; Galatians 4:6; Ephesians 2:20-22; Second Timothy 1:14; and Ezekiel 36:27.

2. Jesus said, "…The mouth speaks what the heart is full of" (Luke 6:45 *NIV*). That is why He wants our entire being flooded and filled with His Holy Spirit. According to First Corinthians 14:4; Jude 20; and Ephesians 6:18, what are you to do regularly to receive fresh infillings of the oil of the Spirit? If you haven't received this gift the Bible calls the *baptism in the Holy Spirit* and you want to, follow Jesus' instructions in Luke 11:9-13 and call RENNER Ministries at 1-800-742-5593.

PRACTICAL APPLICATION

> But be ye doers of the word, and not hearers only,
> deceiving your own selves.
> — James 1:22

1. What is your reaction to learning that the word "candle" — the Greek word *luchnos* — is not a traditional wax candle but *an oil-burning lamp*? How does this meaning help you better understand what Jesus means when He compared us to candles that are to light the world?

2. When you hear that every building in the First Century — from the smallest house to the greatest palace — depended on oil-burning lamps to provide light, how do you think that applies to you as the *lamp of the Lord* in the Twenty-First Century?

3. There are several features of a First Century oil lamp, which we have listed below. In your own words, describe the spiritual significance for each and how it relates to you as the "lamp of the Lord."

Oil Lamp Feature	Spiritual Significance/Parallel to You as the Lord's "Lamp"
Oil Reservoir —	_____
Spout or Mouth —	_____
Wick or Tongue —	_____
The 'Fire' (and Oil) —	_____

LESSON 3

TOPIC

Quit Badgering Yourself

SCRIPTURES

1. **Matthew 5:15** — Neither do men light a candle, and put it under a bushel, but on a candlestick; and it giveth light unto all that are in the house.

2. **2 Corinthians 4:7** — But we have this treasure in earthen vessels, that the excellency of the power may be of God, and not of us.

GREEK WORDS

1. "candle" — λύχνος (*luchnos*): an oil-burning lamp that is carried by hand, positioned on a table, or elevated on a stand; such lamps were fashioned of earthen clay with a reservoir to hold oil and a wick that gave light in darkness once it was lit; oil-burning lamps were vital to life because they were the only source of light in darkness

2. "treasure" — θησαυρός (*thesauros*): a word describing a treasure, a treasury, a treasure chamber, or a place of safekeeping where riches and fortunes are kept; it presents the idea of a specially built room designed to be the repository for massive riches and wealth

3. "earthen vessels" — ὀστράκινος (*ostrakinos*): pottery made of inferior materials; fragile pottery; the word generally represents anything inferior, low-grade, mediocre, shoddy, second-rate, or substandard; the broken shards of pottery that were used for casting votes against citizens who were banished from society; as a result, it meant to ostracize; it is where we get the word ostracize

4. "bushel" — μόδιος (*modios*): a jar or container used to measure grain

SYNOPSIS

As a child, do you remember singing the song "This Little Light of Mine?" It was quite popular for boys and girls for several decades during the Mid-Twentieth Century. Based on Jesus' declaration in Matthew 5:14 and 15, it encouraged children not to hide their light under a bushel. But what exactly did Jesus mean by that? What is a *bushel*, and why did He say we are to put our light on a lampstand? The answers to these questions and others will be what we focus on in Lesson 3.

The emphasis of this lesson:

To hide your light under a bushel is to smother the flame of God's gifts and talents in your life. What He's placed in you is valuable and needed, so don't badger or put yourself down any longer. Embrace what God has placed in you. Your uniqueness is needed by others.

First Century Oil-Burning Lamps:
Their Structure, History, and Function

After declaring that we are the "light of the world," Jesus elaborated on His comparison, telling His listeners, which includes us, "Neither do men light a candle, and put it under a bushel, but on a candlestick; and it giveth light unto all that are in the house" (Matthew 5:15). In our last lesson, we learned that the word "candle" is from a form of the Greek word *luchnos*, which depicts *an oil-burning lamp that is carried by hand, positioned on a table, or elevated on a stand.* Such lamps were fashioned of earthen clay with a reservoir to hold oil and a wick that gave light in darkness once it was lit. Oil-burning lamps were vital to life because they were the only source of light in darkness.

Regardless of a lamp's type — Greek, Jewish, or Byzantine Christian — all lamps had the same basic features: a handle; a reservoir for oil; an opening on top to fill and refill it with oil; and a wick that went down the lamp's spout or mouth. These oil-burning lamps were so abundant in the First Century that you could put a shovel in the soil just about anywhere in Israel today and eventually dig one up.

When a lamp began to run low on oil, it could easily be refilled by pouring fresh oil into the hole on top. As long as there was oil in the lamp, the wick — sometimes called the 'tongue' of the lamp — remained drenched in oil and could burn for many hours or days. As it was held in one's hand, the lamp could be carried from room to room, providing light everywhere it was needed.

Although many people think that when Jesus used the word "candle" He was referring to traditional candles made of wax, that is not the case. Wax candles as we know them didn't exist in abundance until around the 1400s. The "candle" Jesus was describing was a *luchnos*, a very common, oil-burning lamp used extensively in the First Century. Considering this fact, we could translate the first part of Matthew 5:15: "Neither do men light an *oil-lamp*, and put it under a bushel…."

Another important detail we discussed about these lamps is that they were made of clay and very fragile. In fact, they were so fragile that if someone picked it up too roughly or squeezed the handle too tightly, the lamp would break. In Jesus' day, these oil lamps had to be handled very carefully, lest they bust or be crushed — causing the oil to spill out and the light to be lost. Oil was quite expensive, so people always tried not to waste it. Hence, lamps were handled with great care.

Are you beginning to see why Jesus used oil lamps to depict us as believers? Although our bodies are truly a miracle created by God — like the oil lamps in His illustration — we are made from the clay of the earth, and we are very fragile. Physically, emotionally, and mentally, we are brittle and can easily break, which is why we need to do our best to take good care of ourselves.

Once you understand that you've been fashioned by God to carry the precious oil of the Holy Spirit, it will make you want to do better at taking care of yourself. If you want to give light for a long time, you have to exercise, eat right, and manage your wellbeing. Like these clay lamps that Jesus was referring to, you are made of the dust of the earth, and even the best of us is fragile.

The 'Treasure' of God's Spirit Is Inside You

If we really stop and think about it, the real miracle is that God would choose to put His Spirit inside us. The apostle Paul was amazed by this truth and wrote about it in Second Corinthians 4:7. He said:

But we have this treasure in earthen vessels….

The words "we have" in Greek is *echoman*, the plural form of the word *echo*, which means *to have*, *to hold*, or *to possess*. The use of this word here is the equivalent of Paul saying, "We *have*, we *hold*, and we *possess* this treasure in earthen vessels…."

This brings us to the word "treasure," which is a form of the marvelous Greek word *thesauros*, and it describes *a treasure, a treasury, a treasure chamber*, or *a place of safekeeping where riches and fortunes are securely kept*. It presents the idea of *a specially built room designed to be the repository for massive riches and wealth*. Paul used this word *thesauros*, translated here as "treasure," to describe two things:

- What we *have*.
- Who we *are*.

Friend, you are a *thesauros* — you are a treasury! You are a repository for massive riches! You are a place of safekeeping where God's riches are securely kept. God has created you to be one of His treasure chambers that holds and possesses the priceless oil of the Holy Spirit. How amazing is that!

Moreover, this word *thesauros* is where we get the English word for a *thesaurus*, which is *a treasury of words*. It is words on top of words all used to describe one thing. When we apply this meaning to the word "treasure" in Second Corinthians 4:7, it indicates there are not enough words in the world's vocabulary to describe the matchless treasure God has placed inside us.

Paul Compares Us to 'Earthen Vessels'

Now, if we stopped with the word "treasure" — the Greek word *thesauros* — that would be amazing by itself. But Paul went on to say, "But we have this treasure *in earthen vessels...*" (2 Corinthians 4:7). The phrase "earthen vessels" is translated from a form of the Greek word *ostrakinos*, which describes *pottery made of inferior materials* or *fragile pottery*.

Generally, the word *ostrakinos* represents *anything inferior, low-grade, mediocre, shoddy, second-rate*, or *substandard*. History tells us that the broken shards of this pottery were used for casting votes against citizens who were banished from society. This practice became known as *ostracizing* someone. Hence, the word *ostrakinos* is where we get the English word *ostracize*.

What is interesting about these "earthen vessels" is that they were highly decorated, and yet very inexpensive. If a piece was broken, it was no big deal. You weren't losing something valuable. The fact is, you could go out and get another one just like it. Although this shoddy, First Century pottery was made of inferior materials, it was easily replaceable.

What Does All This Mean to You?

The fact of the matter is that even the best of us is inferior. Our bodies are fragile, mediocre, and they break. As we get older and gravity begins to do its work, things that once stood firmly in place begin to sag and fall. Wrinkles and age spots develop, and we can't do all that we used to do when we were younger.

The inferiority of our "earthen vessels" is what fuels the cosmetic surgery industry today. If you think about it, all of us are trying to fix what is failing in some way. Women apply cosmetics to their faces, men attempt to regrow hair on their heads, and multitudes take health supplements and pharmaceuticals all in an effort to recapture youth and hold back the hands of time.

Paul used this illustration of cheaply made pottery to epitomize us. That explains his amazement that God would place His Spirit in us. When he said, "But we have this treasure in earthen vessels…" (2 Corinthians 4:7), it is the equivalent of him saying, "Can you imagine it? We have, we hold, and we possess this immense and indescribable treasure in these inferior vessels in which we live."

Think of what a miracle it is that God would deposit His Holy Spirit inside us!

In a similar way, Jesus likened us to a "candle," which was a fragile oil lamp. Yet that clay lamp contained valuable oil that empowered the light. Again, in both the Old and New Testaments, oil is the symbol of the Holy Spirit. Just like the fragile, clay lamps to which Jesus referred, God has placed His Spirit in our fragile human forms.

Although at times we feel weak, as long as we yield to the Lord, spending time in His presence and in His Word, He will continually resupply us with enough of the Holy Spirit's oil to keep us burning through the night so we can give light to those who are in darkness around us. God's presence in our lives gives us a continual supply of the oil and the fire of the Holy Spirit!

Rather Than Hide Your Light, Jesus Wants You To Let It Shine

Returning to Jesus' words in Matthew 15:5, He said, "Neither do men light a candle [an oil lamp], and put it under a bushel…." The word "bushel" here is a form of the Greek word *modios*, which describes *a jar or container used to measure grain*. Thus, to put your candle *under a bushel* is like covering your flame with a jar or container.

Just imagine lighting a small, two-inch votive candle and then covering it with a glass mason jar. What will happen? That's right — the flame will slowly go out because oxygen, which fuels the flame, has been cut off. Hence, *to put your candle under a bushel* is to smother the flame of God's light in your life.

Do you see what a powerful statement Jesus was making? He was driving the point home that it makes no sense to light an oil lamp and then put it under a container where no one can see it and it will eventually be extinguished. Why would anyone want to do that?

By using this example, Jesus is admonishing us to keep our gifts, talents, and influence out in the open where they can grow, be seen, and provide light to others. Why would God give you gifts to benefit others and then have you hide them where no one can see them or appreciate them? God never intended for you to conceal your gifts or to hide your influence. He wants your light to shine brightly!

Maybe you've seen yourself as being inferior or maybe the devil has assaulted your self-image and tempted you to wrongly believe that you have nothing to offer. Perhaps you have felt that you fall short in comparison to others whose gifts and talents shine especially brightly.

The truth is, if you've been keeping your gifts and talents under wraps, you may be shocked to discover how gifted and talented you really are — and how much potential influence is inside you just waiting to be tapped. You just need to give yourself the opportunity to shine!

It's time for you to come out of hiding! God put His Spirit and supernatural abilities inside you — and that truth alone should bring you out into the open. His Spirit in you is a rich reservoir of oil that will burn long and burn brightly. You have what it takes to be a success!

Be God's Illuminating Force to the People Around You

Friend, for you to be the phenomenal success and influence God knows you can be, you must quit putting yourself down and choose to step out of the shadows! If you refuse to bring your gifts and talents out from under wraps, no one will ever know what God has put in you. And if you neglect your God-given endowments too long, eventually they will begin to diminish just like a fire that eventually goes out due to lack of oxygen.

Now is the time to get out from under that bushel where you've been hiding and let the Holy Spirit ignite the wick of your life with His fire! If you're willing to keep yielding to the Spirit, He will keep filling and supplying you with enough oil to burn long and strong so you can be a source of light and illumination to many people all the days of your life.

Don't buy into the devil's lies and badger yourself with thoughts that say you have nothing to offer! That is a waste of time. God's Spirit lives in you, and if you'll dare to let Him do it, He will burn so brightly in your life that you will become an illuminating force to people all around you.

So make the decision to get out of the box of insecurity and complacency that has contained you! Stop telling yourself you are not as good or talented as others and start using what God has given you for His glory. As you press into Him and put your wick down deep into the oil of the Holy Spirit, you'll become so saturated with His presence that you'll begin to burn brighter and brighter for Jesus. You've got everything it takes to be all God intended you to be!

In Lesson 4, we will explore how putting your light "on a lampstand" multiplies your reach and effectiveness. The higher your light, the greater that light will be.

STUDY QUESTIONS

> Study to shew thyself approved unto God, a workman that
> needeth not to be ashamed, rightly dividing the word of truth.
> — 2 Timothy 2:15

1. Without question, God has gifted YOU with special abilities so that you can express His love, goodness, and all that He is to others. Consider these amazing truths from God's Word:

   - **In his grace, God has given us different gifts for doing certain things well....**
     — Romans 12:6 (*NLT*)

   - **Each person is given something to do that shows who God is: Everyone gets in on it, everyone benefits. All kinds of things [gifts] are handed out by the Spirit, and to all kinds of people....**
     — 1 Corinthians 12:7,8 (*MSG*)

   - **God has given each of you a gift from his great variety of spiritual gifts. Use them well to serve one another.**
     — 1 Peter 4:10 (*NLT*)

   - **A man's gift makes room for him, and brings him before great men.**
     — Proverbs 18:16 (*NKJV*)

- …A man can receive nothing [he can claim nothing, he can take unto himself nothing] except as it has been granted to him from heaven. [A man must be content to receive the gift which is given him from heaven; there is no other source.]

  —John 3:27 (*AMPC*)

What is the Holy Spirit showing you about the gifts God gives and what He has given to you?

2. In Matthew 25:14-30, Jesus tells us the parable of the talents in which two servants used their gifts, and one "hid his gift" in the ground all his life. What did the two faithful servants do? What consequences did the unfaithful servant reap as a result of not bringing his gifts and talents out into the open to allow them to grow and benefit others? What is the Holy Spirit speaking to you through this example?

3. Do you have an idea of what *your* gifts and talents are? In what ways has God uniquely equipped you to help others and at the same time represent Him? To help you discover and confirm how God has wired you, *pray*. Say, "Father, please show me and confirm to me the gifts and talents You've placed inside me. Show me the reasons people tend to come to me for help. What am I good at doing — that I enjoy doing — that enables me to be a blessing to others?"

PRACTICAL APPLICATION

But be ye doers of the word, and not hearers only,
deceiving your own selves.
—James 1:22

1. In Second Corinthians 4:7, the Bible likens us to "earthen vessels," which describes highly decorated, inferior pottery that is very fragile. How does this imagery help you understand the need to value and take good care of yourself? In what areas of your life do you really need to come up higher and begin to take better care of yourself?

2. Jesus' admonishment not to "put our light under a bushel" is Him telling us not to cover up and smother the flame of His Spirit inside us. Be honest — are you doing this in your life? Are you in a place where it seems your gifts are being smothered and can't get the "oxygen" of His Spirit? What practical and spiritual steps can you take to bring your gifts, talents, and influence out in the open where they can be seen, grow, and provide great benefit to others?

TOPIC

Guts and Gumption

SCRIPTURES

1. **Matthew 5:15** — Neither do men light a candle, and put it under a bushel, but on a candlestick; and it giveth light unto all that are in the house.

GREEK WORDS

1. "candle" — λύχνος (*luchnos*): an oil-burning lamp that is carried by hand, positioned on a table, or elevated on a stand; such lamps were fashioned of earthen clay with a reservoir to hold oil and a wick that gave light in darkness once it was lit; oil-burning lamps were vital to life because they were the only source of light in darkness

2. "candlestick" — λυχνία (*luchnia*): an elevated stand on which an oil lamp is placed; oil-burning lamps were placed on elevated stands so they could give maximum light; it was customary for homes, palaces, businesses, and public buildings to place brightly burning lamps on pedestals because a higher position provided superior light that could illuminate the entire environment

SYNOPSIS

Now more than ever, believers need a holy boldness to stand for what is right and be a beacon of truth and hope to the people of the world. As Christ's ambassadors, we are to be "…bold as a *lion*" (Proverbs 28:1). In other words, those of us who are the righteousness of God in Jesus are to have the guts and gumption to hold back the hordes of darkness and move God's plan forward in these final hours.

So far in this series, we have learned that Jesus has called us to be the light of the world, and rather than hide our light, we are to place it on a candlestick so that it provides light to everyone around us. In this lesson, we will discover the reasons for elevating our light and the wonderful blessing that happens as a result.

The emphasis of this lesson:

To put our lamp on a candlestick as Jesus said means to lift our light — and the light of the Gospel — as high as possible so it can produce its maximum effect. Once elevated, the light becomes so great that more and more people can see, appreciate, and receive the benefits of all our light provides.

Don't Hide Your 'Candle' Under a 'Bushel'

In Lessons 2 and 3, we focused on the first part of Matthew 5:15, where Jesus said, "Neither do men light a candle, and put it under a bushel, but on a candlestick; and it giveth light unto all that are in the house."

We saw that the word "candle" is from a form of the Greek word *luchnos.* It depicts *an oil-burning lamp that is carried by hand, positioned on a table, or elevated on a stand.* Lamps of this kind were fashioned of earthen clay with a reservoir to hold oil and a wick that gave light in darkness once it was lit. Oil-burning lamps were vital to life because they were the only source of light in darkness.

Regardless of whether the lamp was used by Greeks, Jews, or Byzantine Christians, they all had the same basic features: a handle so they can be carried and directed; a reservoir for oil; a hole at the top so it can be filled and refilled with oil; a spout or mouth at one end; and a wick that went down into the lamp so that it could be saturated with oil and lit with fire to bring light everywhere it was taken.

That is what Jesus said *you* are — a spiritual lamp designed to carry light into every place you enter. Just as no one would light an oil-burning lamp and then cover it with a bushel, you are to not hide the light that's in you.

We learned that the word "bushel" in Matthew 5:15 is a form of the Greek word *modios.* It depicts *a jar or container used to measure grain.* When Jesus said that no one lights a candle and then puts it under a bushel, He was telling us not to smother our God-given gifts, talents, and influence by hiding them where no one can see or appreciate them.

Just as it makes no sense to light an oil lamp and put it under a container where it is unseen and will quickly be snuffed out due to a lack of oxygen, God never intended for you to conceal your gifts in secret or hide your influence. Instead, He urges you to keep your gifts, talents, and influence out in the open where they can be seen, grow, and provide benefit to others.

Placing Your Light on a Lampstand Maximizes Its Potential

Rather than hide the light of our life, Jesus said we are to put it "…on a candlestick; and it giveth light unto all that are in the house" (Matthew 5:15). In this verse, the word "candlestick" is a form of the Greek word *luchnia*, and it describes *an elevated stand on which an oil lamp is placed.*

In the ancient world, oil-burning lamps were placed on elevated stands so they could give maximum light, and it was customary for homes, palaces, businesses, and public buildings to place brightly burning lamps on pedestals because a higher position provided superior light that could illuminate the entire environment. The higher the lamp was placed, the brighter the light that was produced.

So, in Matthew 5:15, when Jesus says to put our lamp on a candlestick, He is telling us to lift our light — and the light of the Gospel — as high as possible so it can produce its maximum effect. Once elevated, the light becomes so great that more and more people can see, appreciate, and receive the benefits of all that light provides.

The Lower Your Light, the Lesser the Impact

Now, the opposite is also true. The lower the light, the lesser the impact that light has. If you place a lamp on a table, it will provide light and illumination for those gathered around the table. Likewise, if you put a lamp in the corner, it's going to provide light to those that are in the corner. The lower the light, the less the impact.

But if you elevate that same lamp by putting it on a pedestal, the light — that previously only illuminated a handful of people around a table or in a corner — will begin to impact everyone in the room. The amount of light produced is the same, but the elevated position of the lamp makes the light much more effective. In fact, in the ancient world, people would even hang oil-burning lamps from the ceiling, giving the appearance of what looked like modern-day lights. When they did this, a great deal more people and the area itself benefited from the light produced.

Again, metaphorically speaking, if you keep your light at table level, you'll limit your illumination to the people around the table. If you keep it in the corner, you'll only illuminate people who are in the corner. But if you lift your light high and elevate it by putting it on a pedestal and making it more visible, it will illuminate everyone in the room.

So, when Jesus said, "Neither do men light a candle, and put it under a bushel, but on a candlestick," indirectly, He is asking us, "What kind of impact do you want to make? Do you want to hide your light and have *no* impact? Do you want to have *minimal* impact and just reach people who are close by you? Or do you really want to *maximize* your impact?"

If your answer is to reach as many people as you can, then there is only one way. You must put your light on a candlestick, elevating it to the highest place possible so that "…it giveth light unto all that are in the house" (Matthew 5:15).

If you've got the guts and the gumption to take a stand, you will find that your light — which is your gifts, talents, and influence — will impact a much greater number once it's elevated. Remember, the amount of light given is the same, but the elevated position of the light makes it much more effective.

When Rick Elevated His 'Light,' the Holy Spirit Moved

Rick is certainly no stranger to operating on guts and gumption. Through-out his decades of being in ministry, there have been many times he had to push past fear and intimidation and overcome challenges to see his gifts and talents really make an impact. The story of his first book is a perfect example. Here is what Rick shared:

> Years ago, just after I was filled with the Holy Spirit in 1974, I knew God wanted me to write books that would be read around the world. I thought and dreamt about it constantly. Then when I was about 15 or 16 years of age, I began writing my first book, which was titled *The Perfect Gift*.

Believe it or not, it was all about fivefold ministry and how Christ expresses Himself to the Church through the offices of the apostle, prophet, evangelist, teacher, and pastor (*see* Ephesians 4:11,12). After working on the book for about a year, I entered the university and landed a job in the journalism department. There I learned how to use typesetting equipment and incorporated that knowledge into typesetting my book.

At that point, I was about 17 and had a lot of guts and gumption. So much so that I sent a printed copy of my book to a well-known Christian author. He wrote me back and said he really wanted to talk with me about it.

Per his request, I called him, and immediately he began to tell me how the book was filled with so much revelation, and it was very impactful. But as we talked on, he could hear in my voice that I was very young, which moved him to ask, 'How old are you, Rick?'

'Sir, I'm 17,' I responded.

Suddenly, his whole demeanor changed, and he became indignant.

'How dare you attempt to write a book like this at age 17,' he snarled. 'Why, you're not even old enough to know what life is about.'

The man's response was so strange. Before he knew I was 17, the book held the greatest revelation he had ever read on the subject of fivefold ministry. Once he learned I was 17, it became one of the most repulsive things he'd ever seen.

Needless to say, his negative outburst against me was quite damaging. In fact, after that conversation, I decided I would never write another book. This was the equivalent of me taking my God-given talent and calling and hiding it under a bushel. Several years passed, and my gift remained concealed in secret, even though I knew in my heart God had called me to write.

Then one day I had the opportunity to preach for Bob Yandian, who was my pastor in the United States at that time and whom I loved and greatly respected. When I was done with the message, he turned and said to me, 'Rick, what you've just preached in my church is so powerful that you need to put it into a book.'

A book? I thought. *You've got to be kidding. The last time I attempted to write a book I was lambasted by someone I respected.*

Although I was not very excited, I submitted to his instruction because he was my pastor. I began writing a book entitled, *Seducing Spirits and Doctrines of Demons*, which is now no longer in print. Once I made the decision to begin writing, I said to myself, *If I'm going to write a book and invest in printing the book, which costs a lot of money, then I need to lift my light and do something to elevate the book, so people know about it. Otherwise, it's just going to affect a handful of people that I know.*

Well, back in those days, the best place to advertise a Christian book was *Charisma Magazine*. So even though it was quite expensive, I bought a full-page ad for several months, and what happened was miraculous! When I lifted my light and began to make the book known, God moved, and people everywhere began buying the book. Within 30 days, my book, *Seducing Spirits and Doctrines of Demons*, became a bestseller!

After we completely ran out of the first printing, we did a reprint — and then another reprint and another reprint. What would have happened had I only made that book available to those around me? It would have affected only a few people. For my dream to come to pass, I had to accept that my light was needed in the lives of other people, and then I had to elevate it out of the shadows and allow God to use it in His perfect timing to edify and bless others.

It's been many years since that book was released, and to date, God has enabled Rick to write 58 books, with several more on the way! It's so good that Rick had the guts and the gumption to take the risks and elevate that first book — his God-given light — and promote it on one of the highest "lampstands" he could find. Had he not done that, chances are most people would have never known about or benefitted from the gift of writing on his life.

What's Your Story?

One thing is clear, and that is you've got talent! God has gifted you with unique abilities that are meant to be a blessing to countless others. The Bible says, "God has given each of you a gift from his great variety of spiritual gifts. Use them well to serve one another" (1 Peter 4:10 *NLT*).

Maybe you can sing or maybe you can write. It may be that you have been gifted with remarkable administrative skills, a powerful teaching ability, or a divine knack for generating finances as a successful businessperson. Whatever your gifts are, are you using them? If so, how many people are you affecting?

Are you keeping your light low on the table or in a small corner, metaphorically speaking, so just a few folks are affected? Or do you have enough guts and gumption to lift your light high on a lampstand? The idea of promoting your gift might seem audacious, and there very well may be others that are more gifted than you.

Rick himself said that there are much better writers than him, but those writers are not known because they never had the guts and gumption to elevate their gift so that the masses could see it. Consequently, their books are in boxes in their basements or garages, and they've only affected a few people.

Today, Jesus is still saying what He declared in Matthew 5:15:

> **Neither do men light a candle, and put it under a bushel, but on a candlestick; and it giveth light unto all that are in the house.**

Think of how deeply satisfying it would be for you to know that people in your home, at work, at school, in your church, and in all spheres of your life were blessed because you let your light shine!

Friend, God has given you everything you need to make that kind of difference in the lives of others, but you are the only one who can decide to put that light up on a lampstand where it will be a blessing to others. No one can make that decision for you.

If you want to have an impact on many people, you must come out from the shadows and stop concealing the gifts and talents God has given you. Instead, dare to lift your light high so it can shine brightly in the open for everyone to see it and be affected by it. With the empowerment of the oil and fire of the Spirit in your life, your elevated light will make a difference in others!

STUDY QUESTIONS

> Study to shew thyself approved unto God, a workman that needeth not to be ashamed, rightly dividing the word of truth.
> — 2 Timothy 2:15

1. Intimidation and fear are often the biggest barriers that hinder us from fully functioning in our gifts and making the greatest impact for God. When Timothy was faced with fear, Paul wrote to him and told him how he needed to handle it. Carefully reflect on what Paul said and write down how his instructions might apply in your life and situation.

   • **Do not neglect the gift which is in you, [that special inward endowment] which was directly imparted to you [by the Holy Spirit] by prophetic utterance when the elders laid their hands upon you [at your ordination]. Practice and cultivate and meditate upon these duties; throw yourself wholly into them [as your ministry], so that your progress may be evident to everybody.**
   — 1 Timothy 4:14,15 (*AMPC*)

   • **This is why I remind you to fan into flames the spiritual gift God gave you when I laid my hands on you. For God has not given us a spirit of fear and timidity, but of power, love, and self-discipline. So never be ashamed to tell others about our Lord....**
   — 2 Timothy 1:6-8 (*NLT*)

2. Rick shared how someone's criticism of him and the very first book he wrote caused him to stop using his gift for many years. Can you identify with what he went through? Has criticism from others — especially those you admire — caused you to put your gifts and talents under wraps? If so, briefly share what took place — and how God helped you break free from the pain and move forward again.

PRACTICAL APPLICATION

> But be ye doers of the word, and not hearers only,
> deceiving your own selves.
> — James 1:22

1. Rather than hide the light of your life, Jesus said you are to *put it on a candlestick* so that it can produce its maximum potential. What position best describes the location of your light (gifts, talents, influence)? Is it under a bushel? In a corner? On a table? Or high up on a lampstand?

2. In a practical sense, what might it look like to "place your light on a lampstand?" In other words, in what realistic ways might you elevate your influence, your talents, and what you bring to the world so that you can maximize your impact? Pray and ask the Lord, "What can I do to raise my life's light so it can benefit and be a blessing to more and more people?"

LESSON 5

TOPIC

You Are Golden

SCRIPTURES

1. **Matthew 5:15** — Neither do men light a candle, and put it under a bushel, but on a candlestick; and it giveth light unto all that are in the house.

2. **2 Corinthians 4:7** — But we have this treasure in earthen vessels, that the excellency of the power may be of God, and not of us.

3. **Revelation 1:12** — ...And being turned, I saw seven golden candlesticks.

4. **Ephesians 5:26,27** — That he [Jesus] might sanctify and cleanse it [the Church] with the washing of water by the word, that he might present it to himself a glorious church, not having spot, or wrinkle, or any such thing; but that it should be holy and without blemish.

GREEK WORDS

1. "treasure" — θησαυρός (*thesauros*): a word describing a treasure, a treasury, a treasure chamber, or a place of safekeeping where riches and fortunes are kept; it presents the idea of a specially built room designed to be the repository for massive riches and wealth

2. "earthen vessels" — ὀστράκινος (*ostrakinos*): pottery made of inferior materials; fragile pottery; the word generally represents anything inferior, low-grade, mediocre, shoddy, second-rate, or substandard; the broken shards of pottery that were used for casting votes against citizens who were banished from society; as a result, it meant to ostracize; it is where we get the word ostracize

3. "golden" — χρυσός (*chrusos*): gold; the most valuable material that existed in the ancient world; it denotes that which is rare and highly prized; it can be used figuratively to denote something precious or of great significance

SYNOPSIS

When God looks at you, what does He see? Is it a catalog of all your past failures? Is it a two-column ledger with all your mistakes and weaknesses listed on the left and all your godly qualities and good deeds on the right? How you believe God sees you is vital to the health of your soul and spirit and how effective you are at letting your light shine for Him.

The truth is, if you have surrendered your life to Christ, when God the Father looks at you, He sees Jesus! Your life is "hidden in Christ," you are a "new creation," and in His eyes you are "golden"! (*See* Colossians 3:3; 2 Corinthians 5:17; Revelation 1:12.)

The emphasis of this lesson:

In Jesus' eyes, we are golden because He paid for us with His own life's blood and has deposited within us His precious Holy Spirit. Even though we have imperfections and weaknesses, He calls us golden and places immense value on us, His Church. Our refining process is still in progress, and the Spirit will continue His work in us until Jesus returns.

A Review of Matthew 5:15

In the four previous lessons, we have unpacked the meaning of what Jesus said in Matthew 5:15. Immediately after declaring that we as believers are the *light of the world*, He stated:

> **Neither do men light a candle, and put it under a bushel, but on a candlestick; and it giveth light unto all that are in the house.**

As a quick review, here are the meanings of the three key words in this verse that we've studied:

The word "candle" is a form of the Greek word *luchnos*. Unlike traditional wax candles that didn't exist in abundance until around the 1400s, this word *luchnos* depicts *an oil-burning lamp that is carried by hand, positioned on a table, or elevated on a stand*. Lamps of this kind all had the same basic features: a handle so they can be carried and directed; a reservoir for oil; a hole at the top so it can be filled and refilled with oil; a spout or mouth at one end; and a wick that went down into the lamp so that it could be saturated with oil and lit with fire to bring light everywhere it was taken.

The word "bushel" is a form of the Greek word *modios*. It depicts *a jar or container used to measure grain*. When Jesus said that no one lights a candle and then puts it under a bushel, He was literally saying that no one lights an oil lamp and then covers it with a container. The container would smother and snuff out the flame because it would cut off the supply of oxygen.

The spiritual parallel here is that we are not to conceal the God-given gifts, talents, and influence on our life. It is a flame fueled by the oil of the Holy Spirit who lives within us. Instead of hiding our light, God wants us to keep our gifts, talents, and influence out in the open where they can grow, be seen, and be a great blessing in the lives of others.

The word "candlestick" is a form of the Greek word *luchnia*. This term describes *an elevated stand on which an oil lamp is placed*. In the ancient world, oil-burning lamps were put on pedestals so they could give maximum light. This practice was customary in homes, palaces, businesses, and public buildings. The higher the light was positioned, the greater the illumination to the entire environment.

The opposite is also true: the lower the light, the lesser the impact that light has. If you place a lamp on a table, it will provide illumination for those gathered around the table. Likewise, if you put a lamp in a corner, it will provide light to those that are in the corner. Again, the lower the light, the lesser the impact.

So, when Jesus says, "Neither do men light a candle, and put it under a bushel, but on a candlestick" (Matthew 5:15), He is telling us to lift our light — and the light of the Gospel — as high as possible so it can produce its maximum effect. Once elevated, the light becomes so great that more and more people can see, appreciate, and receive the benefits that light provides.

If you've got the guts and the gumption to take a stand, you will find that your light — which is your gifts, talents, and influence — will impact a much greater number of people once it's elevated. Remember, the amount of light given is the same, but the elevated position of the light makes it much more effective. The higher the light, the greater the light, and the greater the impact.

We *Have*, We *Hold*, and We *Possess* Immense, Imaginable Treasure!

Now, if you're struggling with feeling inferior, you need to be reminded of what the Bible says in First Peter 1:18 and 19. Here, Peter declares that you are so valuable Jesus died for you and paid for you with His own life's blood! Add to this, the unbelievable miracle that God has chosen to place His Spirit inside you!

We saw in Lesson 3 that the apostle Paul was so amazed by this truth that he wrote about it in Second Corinthians 4:7, telling us:

But we have this treasure in earthen vessels....

The phrase "we have" in Greek is *echoman*, which is the plural form of the word *echo*, and it means *to have*, *to hold*, or *to possess*. According to this amazing verse, we *have*, we *hold*, and we *possess* treasure in earthen vessels.

The word "treasure" is also significant. It is a translation of the remarkable Greek word *thesauros*, and it describes *a treasure, a treasury, a treasure chamber*, or *a place of safekeeping where riches and fortunes are securely kept*. It presents the idea of a specially built room designed to be the repository for massive riches and wealth.

The fact that Paul used this word *thesauros*, translated here as "treasure," means that *you* — your physical body — is a specially built container designed to be the repository for massive spiritual riches and wealth. You are a *thesauros* — a treasure, a treasury, and a treasure chamber! You are a place of safekeeping where God's riches are securely kept, and those riches include the precious oil of the Holy Spirit.

In Spite of Our Frailties and Flaws, God Chooses To Fill Us With His Spirit

Looking again at Paul's words in Second Corinthians 4:7, he said, "But we have this treasure *in earthen vessels*...." We learned that the phrase "earthen vessels" is derived from the Greek word *ostrakinos*, which describes *pottery made of inferior materials* or *fragile pottery*.

In general, the word *ostrakinos* denotes *anything inferior*, *low-grade*, *mediocre*, *shoddy*, *second-rate*, or *substandard*. History tells us that the broken shards of this pottery were used for casting votes against citizens who were banished from society. This procedure became known as *ostracizing* someone. Hence, the word *ostrakinos* is from where we get the English word *ostracize*.

People loved these "earthen vessels" because they were very inexpensive. If a piece got broken, it was no big deal, because you could go out and get another one just like it. It was easily replaceable. Although this inferior pottery had many flaws, those imperfections were covered over with very colorful, decorative paint that was pleasing to the eye.

Like this shoddy pottery, we too have many faults and imperfections, and we attempt to cover them in all kinds of ways. From costly clothing and cosmetics to Botox and plastic surgery, we're constantly trying to fix our "earthen vessels" and make ourselves as presentable as possible. Yet despite our frailties and flaws, God has chosen to deposit the fullness of His precious Holy Spirit in us! This is simply amazing!

In Jesus' Eyes, We Are 'Golden'

Now at the moment of salvation, when the Holy Spirit comes and takes up residence inside us, He brings with Him all kinds of gifts, abilities, and endowments. In that instant, we become a treasure chamber of the immense riches of God, and in God's eyes we are "golden."

We see this idea displayed in the first chapter of Revelation. The apostle John, who wrote the book of Revelation while imprisoned on the isle of Patmos, had a vision of Jesus standing in the middle of seven *golden candlesticks* (*see* Revelation 1:12). Here, the word "candlesticks" is a form of the Greek word *luchnia*, the same word we saw translated as "candlestick" in Matthew 5:15.

Hence, the "candlesticks" John saw are *elevated stands on which an oil lamp is placed*. In this case, the seven oil lampstands were fashioned from *gold*. They represent the seven major churches of Asia, which were in Ephesus, Smyrna, Pergamon, Thyatira, Sardis, Philadelphia, and Laodicea.

All seven of these churches had difficulties, and from a natural standpoint, people could see the problems they were facing. But when Jesus stood in the midst of these "candlesticks" or churches, they became *golden* because He had purchased all the people with His own blood and had placed His very own Spirit inside them.

In the same way, we may see ourselves as being shoddy, frail, and full of defects, and we may view the modern Church as having many faults that we don't like. But that doesn't matter because when Jesus looks at us, we sparkle in His eyes! He knows, "[God] hath delivered us from the power of darkness, and hath translated us into the kingdom of his dear Son: In whom we have redemption through his blood, even the forgiveness of sins" (Colossians 1:13,14).

Because Christ paid the highest price to redeem us out of sin and Satan's slavery, we are now *golden*. That's the way John describes the Church in Revelation 1:12. He uses the word "golden," which is a form of the Greek word *chrusos*, and it describes the purest *gold*. This was the most valuable material that existed in the ancient world. Moreover, it denotes *that which is rare and highly prized* and can be used figuratively to denote *something precious or of great significance*.

John used this word *chrusos* — translated here as "golden" — to describe the Church, and since we are members of the Church, we are seen as pure *gold* in Jesus' eyes!

The Reason We Are
Described as 'Golden'

In Rick's book, *A Light in Darkness*, he closely examines John's revelation of Jesus and explains why we are seen and described as "golden." Here is an excerpt to provide greater illumination of gold's value in New Testament times:

> The word 'golden' is from the Greek word *chrusos* — the word for *gold* in both the Septuagint (the Greek version of the Old Testament) and the Greek New Testament. This particular word is used throughout ancient literature to describe the purest form of gold.
>
> Just as is true today, the most sought-after and expensive gold in the ancient world was the gold that was *absolutely pure*. Other forms of this precious metal were less valuable because they were mixed with silver, producing a lower and less desirable grade of gold.
>
> John writes in [Revelation 1:12] that the seven candlesticks [or the seven churches] he saw were "golden." Because he uses the word *chrusos*, we know there was nothing inferior, low-grade, or undesirable about those candlesticks. In God's eyes, they were *pure gold*, fashioned out of the most high-grade, desirable material.
>
> Although gold can be found as solid nuggets, the majority of gold is located in rock that must be mined from the earth, and the process of extracting it has always been long and expensive. First, the rock must be removed from the earth and then crushed into dust. Once the rock is crushed, tons of water wash away the lighter rock and dirt, leaving behind the heavier raw gold. The exposed gold is gathered and placed into a furnace with blazing hot temperatures that melt the precious metal into liquid form....
>
> This refining process is long and laborious, and the heat that must be endured by the gold worker is furiously intense. From beginning to end, the process is tedious, expensive, uncomfortable, and complicated — but it is the only way to produce the *purest gold*.[1]

It is important to note that eliminating impurities in gold without fire is impossible. These imperfections must be removed, otherwise they will weaken the object being created. Rick goes on to say:

> Because of the high cost required to produce this grade of pure, refined gold, it became *the* metal associated with royalty or nobility. In the ancient world, only pure gold was fitting for magnificently wealthy, powerful kings or nobility and was therefore used to make their cups, bowls, plates, saucers, and platters, as well as many other items. When ambassadors or the head of a foreign state came to visit a king, they came with gifts. To bring a gift crafted of gold (*chrusos*) was a way of showing the highest respect and honor....
>
> Thus, pure gold was also a symbol of *glory that never fades*. There was simply nothing more valuable than pure gold at the time the book of Revelation was written. It is therefore very significant that this word [*chrusos*] was used to symbolize the seven churches.[2]

Make no mistake. The fact that the Holy Spirit prompted John to use the word "golden" (*chrusos*) to describe and symbolize the Church in Revelation 1:12 conveys the *immense value* that Jesus places on His Church — which includes *you* and every other Blood-bought believer in Christ.

You and the Church Are Still in the Purification Process

Now we're living in a day when society is very critical of everyone, and a great deal of criticism is constantly being leveled against the Body of Christ — especially on social media. Although many people focus on its failures and weaknesses, it is good for us to remember that Jesus gave His own blood to purchase His Church and that it is valuable and precious to Him.

You, too, may feel upset and disheartened by things you know and have seen happening in the Church. You may even be discouraged because of your own experiences with a local church body and be tempted to think that the modern Church is in an irreversibly sad condition, and it will never turn around for the better.

Whenever your mind is bombarded by such thoughts, remember, Jesus loves His Church, and you are a part of it. Both the Church — and

YOU — are still in the process of purification and refinement by the Holy Spirit. Although you may see yourself as fragile, made of clay, and still battling with imperfections, Jesus sees you and the Church as pure gold.

So when you're tempted to focus on the imperfections in yourself or God's people, think back to the gold worker in the midst of the refining process, scraping impurities off the surface of the hot molten gold. The Church's refining process is still in progress, and the Holy Spirit's fire is working to expose all blemishes in order to bring the Church to a higher level of purification.

Choose To Look Beyond Your Defects and See Yourself the Way God Sees You

Each of us must allow the Holy Spirit's fire to expose our weaknesses, impurities, and defects so Jesus can scrape them away. The Church's imperfections are nothing new, and as long as the Church awaits the coming of Jesus, this refining process will never end. Paul wrote about this in Ephesians 5:26 and 27 saying:

> That he [Jesus] **might sanctify and cleanse it [the Church] with the washing of water by the word, that he might present it to himself a glorious church, not having spot, or wrinkle, or any such thing; but that it should be holy and without blemish.**

Jesus isn't blind to the defects in you or in the Church, but He chooses to see beyond that! He sees the price He paid for you and the treasure of His Spirit living in you, and even with all the glaring problems that are there, He has never abandoned His people.

Friend, you have been designed by God to contain the precious oil of the Holy Spirit. You are an "earthen vessel" in which all the treasure of Heaven rests, and God has designed you to be filled and refilled with the oil of His Spirit.

Like an oil-burning lamp, God has given you a reservoir for His oil, a mouth, and a wick (or tongue) that can be saturated with the oil of the Holy Spirit. He has given you the fire of His Spirit so you can burn brightly for Him and take His fire with you every place you go and dispel the darkness. It is no wonder that Jesus sees you as pure gold!

So rather than badger yourself mentally and verbally and downgrade your gifts and abilities, begin to declare what God declares. Say, "I am divinely gifted, and my life has purpose. I am a treasure chamber for the oil of the Spirit, and He is still at work purifying my life to make me more like Jesus."

Likewise, instead of continuing to smother your light by putting it "under a bushel," bring it out into the open. You can start by putting your light on the table and allowing it to illuminate those around the table. If you feel like you're in a corner, let your light shine and give light to those in the corner. And if you've got guts and gumption, take the next step and lift your light and place it on a pedestal so that you can really begin to influence the lives of many people.

Remember, Jesus will keep working as the Great Refiner — washing you with the water of His Word and allowing the fire of the Holy Spirit to burn away the dross and make you the light He has called you to be! The Bible says, "…He Who began a good work in you will continue until the day of Jesus Christ [right up to the time of His return], developing [that good work] and perfecting and bringing it to full completion in you" (Philippians 1:6 *AMPC*).

STUDY QUESTIONS

Study to shew thyself approved unto God, a workman that needeth not to be ashamed, rightly dividing the word of truth.
— 2 Timothy 2:15

1. As you read through the brief history of gold and the meaning of the Greek word *chrusos*, what new insights did you learn? How do these details help you better understand your value in Jesus' eyes?

2. Just as pure gold is produced from rock that is mined from the earth and rigorously refined, the "gold" in your life is produced by the ongoing refining process of the Holy Spirit working in you. What does this process look like? Check out these *pictures of purification* in Scripture and jot down what the Holy Spirit reveals to you about the work He is doing in your life.

    • He is the *Refiner* — Malachi 3:2 and 3

    • He is the *Potter* — Jeremiah 18:1-6

- He is the *Gardener* — John 15:1-5
- He is the *Father Who Disciplines* — Hebrews 12:5-11
- He is the *Shaker of all things* — Hebrews 12:26-29

3. It is vital to remember that the Holy Spirit is the one who brings transformation — not you. You can learn more about this in First Thessalonians 5:23 and 24; Hebrews 13:20 and 21; Philippians 1:6 and 2:12,13. As you cooperate with Him and yield to His work in your life, you will become like pure gold.

PRACTICAL APPLICATION

**But be ye doers of the word, and not hearers only,
deceiving your own selves.
— James 1:22**

1. According to Revelation 12:10, Satan is called the *accuser of the brethren*, and he is constantly accusing us to God. Do you ever find yourself accusing others — especially fellow believers — of the wrongs they've committed? Or are you constantly finding fault with yourself? If you answered yes to one or both questions, you are doing exactly what the enemy wants. Take time to repent of giving place to a critical, judgmental spirit and ask the Lord to give you His love and grace to allow others (and yourself) to make mistakes and grow in their relationship with Him.

2. If you struggle to see yourself as "golden," what is it about your life that you just can't seem to let go of — what faults, past failures, or weaknesses always seem to be staring at you and screaming for your attention? Surrender these things to God in prayer and ask Him to give you a heart revelation of His unconditional love and forgiveness. (Consider First Corinthians 13:4-8 and First John 4:18 as you answer.)

---

[1] Rick Renner, *A Light in Darkness* (Harrison House Publishers, 2018) pp. 70,71.
[2] Ibid.

A Prayer To Receive Salvation

If you've never received Jesus as your Savior and Lord, now is the time for you to experience the new life Jesus wants to give you! To receive God's gift of salvation that can be obtained through Jesus alone, pray this prayer from your heart:

Jesus, I repent of my sin and receive You as my Savior and Lord. Wash away my sin with Your precious blood and make me completely new. I thank You that my sin is removed, and Satan no longer has any right to lay claim on me. Through Your empowering grace, I faithfully promise that I will serve You as my Lord for the rest of my life.

If you just prayed this prayer of salvation, you are born again! You are a brand-new creation in Christ! Would you please let us know of your decision by going to **renner.org/salvation**? We would love to connect with you and pray for you as you begin your new life in Christ.

Scriptures for further study: John 3:16; John 14:6; Acts 4:12; Ephesians 1:7; Hebrews 10:19,20; 1 Peter 1:18,19; Romans 10:9,10; Colossians 1:13; 2 Corinthians 5:17; Romans 6:4; 1 Peter 1:3

CLAIM YOUR FREE RESOURCE!

As a way of introducing you further to the teaching ministry of Rick Renner, we would like to send you FREE of charge his teaching, "How To Receive a Miraculous Touch From God" on CD or as an MP3 download.

How To Receive a Miraculous Touch From God
Rick Renner
CD36
RENNER

In His earthly ministry, Jesus commonly healed *all* who were sick of *all* their diseases. In this profound message, learn about the manifold dimensions of Christ's wisdom, goodness, power, and love toward all humanity who came to Him in faith with their needs.

☑ **YES, I want to receive Rick Renner's monthly teaching letter!**

Simply scan the QR code to claim this resource or go to: **renner.org/claim-your-free-offer**

Connect

WITH US!

R renner.org

f facebook.com/rickrenner • facebook.com/rennerdenise

▶ youtube.com/rennerministries • youtube.com/deniserenner

◎ instagram.com/rickrenner • instagram.com/rennerministries_
instagram.com/rennerdenise

www.ingramcontent.com/pod-product-compliance
Lightning Source LLC
Chambersburg PA
CBHW071651040426
42452CB00009B/1831